e co ti podají. Lepší kuchyně než apatika

Vitalis

Harald Salfellner

The Best
Czech Recipes

Vitalis

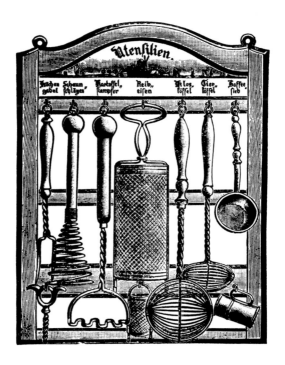

Contents

Introduction

For many people, Old Bohemia, its capital city "Golden Prague" and the peaceful countryside of Moravia conjure up nostalgic images of times gone by. And just as in the days of the Emperor, people flock to the Czech Republic today to savour tasty local specialities, ranging from the fine delicacies of the international spa centres of Karlovy Vary (Carlsbad), Mariánské Lázně (Marienbad) or Františkovy Lázně, to the hearty rustic stews renowned in the Krkonoše (Giant Mountains) and the Šumava (Bohemian Forests).

Bohemian cuisine is fed by two major culinary sources: the German-Czech culinary tradition, characterised by considerable regional variations, naturally dominant in the mostly mountainous border areas, inhabited predominantly by Germans, and Czech-Slavonic customs of cooking and eating, which are still quite distinct from the cuisine of other Slavic countries such as Russia and Poland. A glance at the history of this land is enough to show the range of other influences alongside these important original sources. King Charles IV brought, among other things, wine grapes from Burgundy, Josef Groll introduced Pilsen beer from Bavaria, and the Tyroleans living in Volary brought, if not Tyrolean dumplings, at least something of their Alpine eating habits to South Bohemia. In the 20th century many Slovakian dishes were adopted, and the decades of subordination to the

Soviet Empire also left their mark. This diversity makes Czech cuisine a worthy member of a shared European cultural heritage, which is more than just the sum of national identities and is inspired and nourished by foreign influences.

This little book is a collection of the best recipes both old and new, presented in such a way that they can be easily prepared in the average modern kitchen. We wish you every success with them and "bon appetit", or as we say here: "Dobrou chuť!"

Harald Salfellner

Unless otherwise stated, all recipes serve 4.

Lomnice Cookies (Lomnické suchary)

Heat

250ml milk, (taking care not to scald it) and dissolve

25g yeast in it with a little
sugar. Add
500g flour,
150g butter and
3 egg yolks, working the mixture into a firm dough. Mix

a pinch of salt with a little
grated lemon zest,
½ tsp nutmeg, and
a knife-tip of ground
fennel to the dough. Leave the dough to rise for 30 minutes, then divide into two and roll out. Place on a greased baking tray and leave to rise another 20 minutes. Bake at 200° for about 30 minutes. The following day, cut into slices about a finger thick and leave in the oven at 120° until they have dried out. Toss in

4 packets vanilla sugar while still warm.

Apple Charlotte (Žemlovka)

	Cut
10 dried bread rolls	into thin slices. Whisk together
500ml milk,	
3 eggs	and
100g sugar	and leave the sliced bread to soak in the mixture. Peel and core
750g apples	and slice thinly. Mix with
50g raisins	and
50g slivered almonds.	Place alternate layers of softened bread and fruit into a well greased baking tin. The top layer should be of bread. Dot the top with
50g butter,	pour over the remaining milk and place the baking tin in a pre-heated oven at 200°. Leave to bake for 30 minutes. Then mix
2 egg whites	with
30g sugar	and whisk until thick. Spread the meringue over the top and return it to the oven for 10 minutes or until the top is slightly browned.

Apple Charlotte

Prague Ham Loaf (Pražská šunka)

	Place
80g yeast	in a small bowl and mix with
1 tsp sugar	until the yeast has liquefied. In a large bowl, mix
500g rye flour	with
1 tbsp salt,	
250g wheat flour	and
50g wheatgerm.	Using a fork for this will make sifting unnecessary. Add
600ml water	and the liquefied yeast into the bowl and mix well. Cover the dough and leave to rise. Cook
1kg ham (soaked in water overnight)	on a low heat in a covered pan for about one hour. Remove the skin, and leave the ham to cool. Sprinkle a pastry board with flour and roll out the dough to about 1cm thick. Then whisk
2 or 3 eggs	and spread half on the dough. Carefully wrap the ham in the dough and smooth the edges. Use
75g butter	to grease a large baking tray and place the filled loaf on it. Brush it with the remaining egg and prick the surface with a fork several times. Bake at 225° for about 2½ hours.

Prague Ham Loaf

Tripe Soup (Dršťková polévka)

	Clean
250g tripe	thoroughly and rinse it several times in cold water. Rub with
salt	and clean once more. Then cook, strain and leave to drip, before bringing it to the boil again in fresh water together with some
salt, 1 onion, 1 clove of garlic soup vegetables, marjoram, ginger, sweet paprika pepper.	and all finely chopped. Season to taste with and Leave to simmer on a low heat for about two hours until the tripe is nice and tender. Melt
30g butter 40g flour.	in a pan and whisk in Gradually dilute with the stock. Simmer for 10 to 20 minutes, so that the soup does not taste of flour. Stir well to avoid scorching the roux. Finely chop the tripe and add it to the soup together with
100g diced smoked meat. chopped parsley.	Boil briefly and serve with

Tripe Soup (bottom), Potato Soup (centre), Sauerkraut Soup (top)

Sauerkraut Soup (Zelňačka)

	Dice
40g bacon	and render it down with
20g butter	in a large saucepan. Very finely chop
1 onion	and
2 cloves of garlic	and sweat until transparent, add
2 tsp sweet paprika.	Add
250g sauerkraut	and season to taste with
salt	and
½ tsp caraway seeds.	Add
750ml meat stock	and bring to the boil. Prepare a roux with
50g butter	and
50g flour	and slowly add
750ml meat stock.	Mix the roux in with the soup and simmer for about 15 minutes on a medium heat. Peel and dice
2 potatoes,	add them to the soup and boil for another 15 minutes. Then add.
200g sour cream.	If you wish, you can further spice up your soup with
200g chopped smoked meat or sausage.	

Potato Soup (Bramboračka)

	Finely chop
2 small onions,	
100g carrots,	
50g Hamburg parsley root,	
50g celery	and
1 small leek	into small pieces and sweat them in
20g butter.	Add
500ml salted water	and
500g peeled and diced potatoes.	Simmer for about 25 minutes until nearly done. Season to taste with
½ tsp ground caraway seeds,	
marjoram,	and, if you like, with
1 clove of garlic (crushed).	Heat
70g butter	in a pan and add
70g flour.	Let it foam up and slowly mix in the broth from the potatoes and vegetables. Add the potatoes and vegetables and simmer for another 5 minutes. Finish with
1 tsp butter	and
Maggi seasoning	to taste.

Pickled Herrings Prague Style (Marinovaní sledi)

Serves 8

	Leave
8 salted herrings	to soak for two or three days in plenty of water of water and
a little milk.	Change the liquid frequently, retaining it on the last occasion. Then dry the herrings thoroughly, skin and bone them. Remove the heads and tails and fry the fish in
4 tbsp oil.	Place in a china dish along with
1 bay leaf, green chili peppers, 10 peppercorns onion rings.	and Sieve the liquor in which the herring was soaked and mix with
8 tbsp of cream, oil vinegar	and Pour the sauce over the herrings and leave to stand, covered, for 6 days. This would go well with potato salad, gherkins, capers and baby onions.

PRAKTICKÁ

KUCHAŘKA

OD M. RETIKOVÉ.

CENA 70 HAL.

DRUHÉ DOPLNĚNÉ VYDÁNÍ.

Bohemian Bread Dumplings (Houskové knedlíky)

	Mix
15g yeast	and
1 tsp sugar	until the yeast has liquefied. Pour
400g flour	into a bowl, add the liquid yeast with
1 pinch of salt,	
3 egg yolks,	
125ml milk	and knead it into a dough. Leave to rise for an hour. Cut
1 dry bread roll	into small dice, brown lightly in
40g butter	and when cooled, work into the dough until it is smooth and shiny and no longer sticks to the ladle. Air bubbles will form on its surface that burst as you stir. On a floured pastry board, work the dough into two oblong loaves. Cover with a tea cloth and leave to rise for another 15 minutes. Bring
4l salted water	to a boil in a large saucepan, and place one of the loaves in it. When the water comes back to the boil, carefully lift the dumplings from the bottom and reduce the heat slightly. Boil for 20 minutes, turning the dumplings halfway through. The dumplings are ready when a skewer comes out clean. Remove the dumplings, cut them into thin slices with a string and serve as an accompaniment to a range of dishes.

Bohemian Potato, Bread and Raised Dumplings

Raised Dumplings (Kynuté knedlíky)

	Dissolve
15g yeast	in lukewarm
milk,	add
a little sugar	and let the yeast rise. Mix with
500g coarse-grained	
flour.	Add
1 egg	and
a pinch of salt	and mix thoroughly. Leave to rise for

and mix thoroughly. Leave to rise for an hour and then form into dumplings on a floured pastry board. Cover with a tea cloth and leave to rise again. Simmer the dumplings in a covered saucepan for 15 minutes, then remove the lid and leave the dumplings to cook for another few minutes. Drain well, cut into slices with a string and sprinkle with melted butter.

Potato Dumplings (Bramborové knedlíky)

	Boil
500g floury potatoes	in their skins, peel and grate while still hot. Transfer to a pastry board, form a well in the centre. Add
1 egg, 2 pinches of salt, 80g flour,	and
80g semolina	and work the mixture into a firm dough. Form 5 oblong dumplings and place them all in
4l boiling salted water.	Simmer on a medium heat for 15 minutes. After 8 minutes, turn over carefully. When ready, cut into slices and serve.

Fruit Dumplings (Ovocné knedlíky)

	Mix
15g yeast	with
40g sugar	and
1 pinch of salt	until the yeast has liquefied. Sieve
250g flour	into a bowl and add the liquefied yeast,
1 egg,	
250ml milk	and
1 packet of	
vanilla sugar.	Work the mixture into a dough, sprinkle with flour and leave to rise for 45 minutes. Then roll out the dough thinly and cut into 20 small squares. Stone and wash
20 strawberries or apricots.	If they aren't sweet enough, add a sugar lump in place of the stone. Wrap the fruit in the squares of dough with wet hands and let them rise for another 5-6 minutes. In the meantime, bring
3l salted water	to the boil, divide the dumplings into 4 portions and cook each portion separately for 8-10 minutes on a medium heat. When cooked, remove, prick several times with a fork and set aside in a warm place until all the dumplings are ready. Finally, melt
200g butter	and serve up the dumplings. At the table, sprinkle the dumplings with
150g icing sugar	and
400g grated hard "tvaroh" (Czech curd cheese)	and pour over the melted butter.

Fruit Dumplings

Barley with Mushrooms (Kuba)

	Wash
40g dried mushrooms	in a sieve and soak them, covered, in
500ml water	for 20 minutes. Brown
300g barley	in
40g butter	and pour on
500ml meat stock.	Season with
a pinch of salt	and add the mushrooms with the water used for soaking. Stew, covered, for 50 minutes on a medium heat, stirring occasionally. Peel
2 onions	and
4 cloves of garlic,	chop finely, and sweat in
40g melted butter	until transparent. Add to the barley along with
125ml water,	
1 tsp caraway seeds	and
1 tsp marjoram.	Put the mixture into a greased baking tin, coated with breadcrumbs, and bake uncovered for 15 minutes at 200° in a pre-heated oven. Serve at once.

Barley with Mushrooms (Kuba)

Sauerkraut (Kyselé zelí)

	Finely dice
1 onion	and brown in
50g pork fat.	Add
500g sauerkraut	with its juice, and season with
a pinch of salt	and
1 tsp caraway seeds.	Pour on a little water and boil the sauerkraut until soft. After half an hour, add
1 grated raw potato	and cook on a medium heat for another 15 minutes. Season to taste with
sugar	and
vinegar.	

Spinach Soufflé Pancakes

	Whisk
4 egg yolks	and mix into a light batter with
1 tbsp flour,	
1 tbsp milk,	
1 tbsp water,	
1 pinch of salt	and
1 pinch of nutmeg.	Wash
250g fresh spinach,	chop it finely and mix it into the batter. Whisk
4 egg whites	until thick and fold them into the batter. Then melt
1 tbsp butter	in a frying pan and fry 4 pancakes, 2 minutes on each side. Fold them over and serve with salad.

Bohemian Potato Pancakes (Bramboráky)

	Wash, peel and coarsely grate
1kg potatoes.	Heat
125ml milk	and pour over the potatoes. Mix in
120g flour	and
3 eggs.	Finely dice
100g bacon,	
40g cracklings	and
4 cloves of garlic	and mix with
salt,	
pepper,	
3 tsp marjoram	and
2 tsp ground	
caraway seeds.	Add to the potato mixture and fry the pancakes, one at a time in
100ml oil,	allowing 4-5 minutes for each side. Serve piping hot, straight from the pan.

Potato Pancake

Sour Lentils (Čočka na kyselo)

	Pick over
300g lentils,	wash them in running water, cover with cold water and leave to soak for about 3 hours. Add
2 bay leaves	and cook for 25 minutes on a medium heat, stirring occasionally. Prepare a roux with
30g butter,	
30g flour,	and
250ml meat stock.	Season with
½ tsp salt	and simmer on a medium heat for about 10 minutes, stirring occasionally to prevent scorching. Pour the lentils into the sauce, together with the cooking liquor. Peel and dice
1 onion	and fry it in
50g butter	until golden. Add to the lentils, season with
1 tbsp vinegar	and simmer for another 5 minutes. Finely dice
4 large gherkins	and mix with the lentils before serving. Serve with hard-boiled eggs and fresh bread.

Stuffed Kohlrabi (Plněné kedlubny)

	Peel
4 kohlrabi	and boil for 10 to 15 minutes, acc. to size, in
2l salted water.	Leave the kohlrabi in the cooking liquor to cool. To prepare the stuffing, peel
1 small onion	and
1 clove of garlic,	chop them finely and sweat in
60g butter	until transparent. Clean
100g mushrooms,	slice them thinly and fry briefly with the onion and garlic. Add
150g minced beef	and again fry briefly. Leave the mixture to cool, mix in
1 egg	and season with
salt	and
nutmeg.	When the kohlrabi has cooled, carefully scrape out the flesh and fill with the meat and mushroom stuffing. Grease an ovenproof baking dish with
1 tbsp butter.	Dice the scraped-out flesh, placing it in between the beets. Pour on 300ml of the cooking liquor, cover and bake at 180° in a pre-heated oven. Remove the kohlrabi from the dish and set aside in a warm place. Whisk
2 tbsp flour	with
200ml whipping cream	and pour over the cooked kohlrabi flesh to form a sauce, season with
salt	and
nutmeg.	Bring to the boil and simmer for 10 minutes on a low heat. Purée the sauce and serve with the kohlrabi.

Potato Gnocchi (Škubánky)

	Peel and quarter
1kg potatoes,	and boil in salted water until tender. Strain the potatoes, retaining the water. Mash the potatoes and mix with
150g flour.	Pour on 125ml of the potato water, cover and steam the mixture on the lowest heat. After about 10 minutes, pour off the excess water and stir the mashed potatoes thoroughly. Dip a tablespoon in
50g heated fat.	This makes it much easier to shape the gnocchi and lay them out on a plate. The gnocchi can be served as either a sweet or a savoury dish. For sweet gnocchi, add
ground poppy seeds	and
sugar,	and for a savoury dish, top with
1 onion,	diced and fried.

Potato Gnocchi

Moravian Sparrow (Moravský vrabec)

	Wash and dry
400g side of pork	and
400g shoulder of pork.	Make several cuts in the skin with a sharp knife. Cut each piece of meat into 4 equal portions. Peel and crush
4 cloves of garlic	and mix with
1 tsp salt	and
1 tsp ground caraway seeds.	Rub this paste evenly into the pieces of meat. Peel
4 large onions,	dice and fry in
60g pork fat.	Place the meat skin-side down on the onion and pour over
150ml hot water.	Roast the meat for about 1½ hours, removing the lid after 1 hour. Serve with the cooking juices and onion, accompanied by bread- or potato-dumplings and sauerkraut.

Moravian Sparrow

Spicy Roast Pork (Vepřová pečeně)

	Wash
1-1½kg pork leg,	dry carefully and cut the skin into a diamond-shaped pattern with a sharp knife. Peel and crush
4 cloves of garlic	and mix with
1 tsp salt,	
a little pepper	and
1 tsp caraway seeds.	Rub this mixture into the meat. Quarter
4 bay leaves	and stick them into the cuts in the skin, together with
8 allspice berries,	
8 black peppercorns	and
4 juniper berries.	Briefly sear the joint in a roasting tin, skin-side down, in
5 tbsp oil	and pour over
250ml hot water.	Cover the tin and place in a pre-heated oven at 200° and braise for 2 to 2½ hours. Turn the meat after an hour. Then keep it in a warm place and strain the juice. Stir in
3 tbsp flour,	gradually mix in
250ml water	and simmer on a low heat for 15 minutes. Carve the meat and serve the sauce separately.

Spicy Roast Pork with Dumplings and Sauerkraut

Bohemian Pork Goulash (Vepřový Guláš)

	Dice
750g shoulder of pork.	Heat
5 tbsp oil	in a large casserole dish until extremely hot and sear the meat. Finely dice
1 green pepper,	
4 tomatoes,	
3 large onions	and
2 cloves of garlic	and fry briefly with the meat. Season with
a pinch of salt	and, to taste, with
½ tsp paprika	and
½ tsp caraway seeds.	Pour on
250ml vegetable stock	and cook the goulash for about 45 minutes, until the meat is tender. Remove the dish from the heat and mix in
100g sour cream	into the goulash. Do not allow to boil.

Pork with Beer Sauce (Vepřové v pivní omáčce)

	Clean and dry
1kg shoulder of pork.	Remove the skin and cut the meat into bite-sized pieces. Fry in a casserole in
80g pork fat.	Peel and dice
4 onions	and
4 cloves of garlic,	add them to the casserole, reduce the heat and braise briefly. Season to taste with
salt	and
1 tsp ground caraway seeds.	Add
150ml hot water	and continue to stew on a medium heat for 1½ to 2 hours. At this point, some of the skin may be added to the stew and removed afterwards, but this will make the sauce very greasy. Mix
250ml beer	and
100g breadcrumbs	and season with
pepper.	Add it to the pan juices. Simmer on a low heat for 15 minutes stirring frequently.

Brno Cutlet (Brněnský řízek)

	Wash and dry
4 large pork cutlets.	Cut into thin slices and rub both sides with
4 pinches salt.	Dice
150g cooked ham	and fry in
40g butter.	Beat
3 eggs	and add them to the frying pan. Then add
6 tbsp frozen peas	and stew for about 2 minutes until the mixture thickens. Spread this mixture on the meat slices. Fold them over, holding them together with tooth-picks. Toss the cutlets in
2 tbsp flour.	Beat
2 eggs	with
2 tbsp milk	and dip both sides of the meat into this mixture. Then coat it with
4 tbsp breadcrumbs.	Heat
125ml oil	in a large pan, and slowly fry the cutlets on both sides.

Veal Cutlets in Cream (Telecí řízky na smetaně)

	Wash and carefully dry
4 veal cutlets	and season with
4 pinches salt.	Toss the cutlets in
4 tbsp flour.	Fry in
100g melted butter	for about 5 minutes on each side. Cover pan, and leave cutlets to stew on a low heat for 45 minutes. Prepare a roux from
30g butter,	
30g flour,	
125ml white wine	and
125ml water.	Add
200g whipping cream	and simmer for 15 minutes, stirring constantly. Finely chop
1 sprig of parsley,	
4 anchovies	and
4 tsp capers	and add them to the sauce. Leave the cutlets to marinade in the sauce for another 15 minutes and serve together.

Rabbit with Cream Sauce
(Králík na smetaně)

	Take
1 oven-ready rabbit,	remove all the delicate membrane, clean, cut up and rub with
1 tsp salt.	In a casserole, sear the meat on all sides in
50g butter.	Then reduce the heat to the lowest setting. Quarter
2 large onions	and add them to the meat. Wash, peel and slice
2 carrots, ⅛ of a celeriac root ½ a root of Hamburg parsley.	and

Add them to the casserole and simmer for about 10 minutes. Season with |
| 1 tsp sweet paprika 250ml meat stock. | and add
Put the lid on the casserole and stew for about 2½ hours. Remove the meat and set aside in a warm place, add |
| 200ml whipping cream. | Bring the sauce back to the boil and purée. Return the meat to the sauce and serve. |

Veal Cutlets with Anchovies
(Telecí řízek s ančovičkami)

	Slice
500g veal cutlets (shoulder or leg)	into pieces about a finger thick, tenderise, and season with
salt.	Finely slice
½ onion.	Place onions and meat in a casserole and heat with
40g butter beef stock	until all the juice has evaporated. Add a spoonful at a time until the cutlets are tender. In the meantime grind
2 anchovies butter.	into a mash with some
nutmeg.	Add to the meat and season with Stew the cutlets in the butter until it is as though they are sitting in their own juice. Then toast some
breadcrumbs butter,	in melted dish up the cutlets, sprinkle with the breadcrumbs and garnish with
lemon wedges.	

Carlsbad Roulade (Karlovarská roláda)

	Wash and dry
1½kg oven-ready veal breast	and make a deep incision in the middle. Separate the halves and rub with
4 pinches of salt.	Stuff with
150g cooked ham	and
150g raw ham.	Finely chop
2 gherkins	and sprinkle them over the meat. Then whisk
4 eggs	with
2 pinches of salt	and
2 tbsp milk.	Fry in
2 tsp butter	to make scrambled eggs and spread them over the the meat. Roll the meat up and seal it tightly with meat skewers or butcher's twine. In a roasting tin, brown the meat all over in
60g butter.	Cover the tin, place in a pre-heated oven at 200° and roast meat for about 2½ hours. Turn the meat occasionally and baste with hot water if necessary. Remove the meat and keep it warm, mix
1 tbsp butter	into the pan juices. Add
1 tbsp flour	and
125ml meat stock	or water. Leave the sauce to simmer for 15 minutes on a low heat. Slice the meat and serve in the sauce.

Carlsbad Roulade

Ribs of Lamb in Wine Sauce
(Jehněčí žebírka s vinnou omáčkou)

	Divide
500g rack of lamb	into 4 ribs and slice off the fat and skin. Tenderize the meat and rub well with
1 clove of garlic.	Season with
salt.	Heat
50g fat	in a pan and sweat
1 chopped onion	together with
200g soup vegetables	in it. After about 3 minutes, add the meat. Dice
125g boiled ham	and sprinkle over the lamb ribs. Pour on
250ml white wine	and stew for about 40 minutes until soft. Remove the meat from the pan and transfer to a warmed serving dish. Strain the sauce and pour over the meat.

Ribs of Lamb in Wine Sauce

Roast Sirloin Bohemian Style (Svíčková)

	Clean
1kg sirloin of beef	and remove the skin and sinews. Cut
50g bacon	into strips and lard the meat with them.
	Season sparingly with
salt and pepper.	Then cut or grate
1½kg root vegetables	
(equal quantities of	
carrots, celeriac, and	
Hamburg parsley)	into small pieces. Boil about
1½ l water	in a pan and add
3 bay leaves,	
1 tsp thyme,	
10 allspice berries,	
20 peppercorns,	
salt	and about
150ml vinegar.	Let the marinade cool, place the meat in a roasting tray and pour over the marinade until it is completely covered. Leave to steep overnight in a cool room. On the next day, place it in the oven and roast in the marinade until the meat is tender. Take out the meat, remove the spices and purée the vegetables with the remaining marinade. Add
200ml whipping cream	and season to taste with
sugar	and
lemon	until it is sweet and sour. Carve the meat, pour on the sauce, serve with bread-dumplings and garnish with cranberry jam.

Roast Sirloin Bohemian Style

Sirloin (Roštěná)

	Wash
4 slices of sirloin	in running water and dry them thoroughly. Beat out the slices, make several cuts in the rind and season them with
salt,	
pepper,	
ground caraway seeds	and
4 crushed cloves of garlic.	Toss the meat in
4 tbsp flour	and sear in a cast-iron pan in
80g melted butter,	allowing about 5 minutes for each side. Pour on
125ml meat stock,	cover and stew on a low heat for an hour. Remove the meat and set aside in a warm place, add
200ml sour cream	to the pan juices and bring briefly to the boil. Serve the meat in the sauce.

Sirloin

Roast Goose (Pečená husa)

Serves 8

	Rinse and thoroughly dry
1 oven-ready goose (approx. 4kg).	
salt	Rub with
pepper	and
caraway seeds.	and sprinkle with
1kg cooking apples	Peel and core
1 sprig of thyme	and stuff them into the cavity with
mugwort.	or
	Close the neck and breast with skewers or toothpicks, place the goose breast-side down in a roasting tin. Pour over about
250ml hot water.	Cover, place in a pre-heated oven at 210° and cook for 4 to 6 hours, depending on its size. Turn regularly and baste occasionally with the pan juices. Skim off the excess fat with a ladle into a separate container. Only remove the lid for the last half hour, when the goose is already nice and tender, and brown the skin to a golden colour. Remove the skewers and serve with the pan juices.

Roast Goose

Roast Duck Bohemian Style with Red Cabbage (Kachna s červeným zelím)

	Wash and carefully dry
1 duck (approx. 2½kg)	and rub with
salt	inside and outside. Place it in a roasting tray, add a little
water	and sprinkle the top of the duck with
caraway seeds.	Roast in the oven at around 180°. Halfway though cooking, turn the duck, sprinkle the other side with caraway seeds and roast until tender, keeping the bird covered to prevent it from drying out. Baste with the pan juices from time to time. Towards the end of the cooking time, remove the lid and roast until the duck is crispy.

Red Cabbage

	Pour off half the juice from
2 jars pickled, sweet and sour red cabbage	and reserve it. Place the cabbage in a pan, add
4 cloves	and
4 corns of allspice	and cook gently on a low heat until softened, watching it all the time. Should the liquid evaporate before the cabbage is tender, add the reserved juice and keep simmering. In another pan, sauté a
medium chopped onion	in
pork fat	or the fat from the duck until transparent. Sprinkle with
flour,	add some
water or the marinade	from the cabbage and mix with the cabbage. Season to taste with
salt, sugar and vinegar.	Serve with bread- or potato-dumplings.

Roast Duck Bohemian Style with Red Cabbage

Bohemian Loin of Venison (Srnčí hřbet)

Serves 8

	Remove the skin from
1 loin of venison	and pierce it with a skewer. Cut
150g smoked bacon	into strips and lard the venison with them. Rub it with
salt,	
pepper	and
ground juniper berries.	Heat
120g fat	in a roasting dish and place the venison in it with the larded side down. Cut
1 onion	into rings and spread on the meat, together with
slices of lemon.	Pour the hot fat over the meat and sprinkle with a little
vinegar.	Pre-heat the oven to 200° and cook the venison for 1½ to 2½ hours until tender, according to size. Mix
125ml sour cream	with
a little water	and use to baste the meat from time to time. Halfway though the cooking time, turn the meat and roast the other side until crisp and golden. As soon as the meat is cooked through, remove from the oven, carve and keep warm. Let the pan juices thicken slightly, sprinkle with
20g flour	and allow this to cook down before sieving. Serve the sauce separately.

Bohemian Loin of Venison

Wild Duck with Onion
(Divoká kachna na cibuli)

	Thoroughly clean
1 oven-ready wild duck (approx. 2kg) salt	in running water, dry and season with and
pepper, 3-4 onions,	both inside and outside. Peel and quarter dice them and and stuff them into the cavity together with
1 bay leaf 4 juniper berries.	and Sew up the duck with butcher's twine and truss the wings and legs firmly to the body. Finely slice
300g bacon 60g clarified butter	and cover the duck with them. Heat in a casserole and place the duck in it. Cover the dish, place in a pre-heated oven at 200° and roast the duck for 1½ hours, basting occasionally with some of the juice. Then remove the bacon, uncover the dish and let the duck brown for another 20 minutes. For the sauce, add
2 tbsp flour 250ml white wine 250ml meat stock.	to the pan juices, stir, and slowly add and Simmer the sauce for 10 minutes on a low heat, remove the bay leaves and juniper berries and serve the sauce with the carved duck.

Roast Wild Boar with Juniper Sauce
(Divočák v jalovcové omáčce)

	Clean and carefully dry
1½kg loin of wild boar.	
	Remove skin and sinews, rub with
1 tsp salt	and a little
pepper	to taste. Heat
150g bacon	in a casserole, add the meat and place it in a pre-heated oven at 190°. Leave to stew with the lid on for 2½ hours. If necessary, sprinkle with a little
hot water	from time to time. To prepare the sauce, make a roux using
40g butter,	
40g flour,	
125ml red wine	and
125ml meat stock.	Finely dice
1 small onion	and
100g ham,	and add them to the sauce together with
8 juniper berries.	Bring to the boil and then simmer for 20 minutes, stirring occasionally. Finally, add the pan juices,
200g whipping cream	and season to taste with
1 tsp lemon juice.	Remove the bacon from the pan and slice the meat. Remove the juniper berries from the sauce and pour it over the meat.

Carp with Anchovies (Kapr s ančovičkami)

	Gut and scale
1 carp (approx. 2kg),	wash thoroughly and pat dry. Sprinkle with
50ml lemon juice	and marinade for half an hour. Peel and finely dice
1 onion,	
1 carrot	and
⅛ of a celeriac root	in a saucepan, sauté them in
60g butter	and slake with
125ml wine.	Boil
4 potatoes	peel them and stuff into the belly of the carp. Place the carp on the vegetables, spine upwards, lay
8 anchovies	on top and sprinkle with
2 tbsp breadcrumbs.	Dot with
50g butter	and roast, covered, in a pre-heated oven at 180°, occasionally basting it with the juice. Serve together with the vegetables and potatoes, and extra boiled potatoes on the side.

Carp with Anchovies

Carp in Paprika Sauce (Kapr na paprice)

	Take
1 carp (approx. 2kg),	and scale, gut, wash, fillet and bone it. Cut off the gills and fins and throw away. Put the scraps into a pan with
250ml white wine	and
500ml water.	Add
2-3 onions,	
1 carrot,	
half a leek,	
4 allspice berries	and
2 bay leaves,	and cook for approx. 1½ hours on a low heat. Strain off the stock. Sprinkle the fish fillets with the
juice of one lemon	and leave them to steep for 30 minutes. Peel and dice
1 onion	and sweat it in
60g butter	until transparent. Add
½ tsp sweet paprika,	allow it to foam up, then slowly add the fish stock. Rub
1 tsp salt	into the fillets and stew in the sauce for 15 minutes. Whisk
2 tbsp flour	into
200g cream,	set the fish aside in a warm place and mix the cream into the stock.

Bring to the boil and simmer for 10 minutes, stirring occasionally. Put the fillets on a warmed serving dish, pour the sauce over the top and serve.

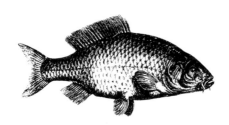

Roast Pike (Pečená štika)

	Clean and skin
1kg pike	so it's ready to cook and rub with
salt.	Sprinkle both inside and outside with the juice of
½ lemon	and sauté in
150g butter.	Roast in the oven at 190°, basting it frequently with butter. Serve the pike garnished with
slices of lemon	and
chopped parsley.	

Tench Bohemian Style (Lín)

Prepare

1 live tench (approx. 1kg)	for cooking. Retain the blood when killing the fish. Soak the fish in boiling water for about a minute to make it easier to scale. Cut the fish into portions, sprinkle with
salt	and leave to stand for an hour. Then heat
100g butter	in a saucepan and sauté the fish slices. Halve
2 onion cloves.	and stud them with Add them to the fish along with the
grated zest of half a lemon 200g celery.	and Cover the pan and stew for 15 minutes. Then turn over the fish slices and sprinkle with
2 tbsp flour. 250ml pea stock 2 tbsp vinegar	Pour onto the fish along with and the retained blood and simmer for another 5 minutes. Strain the sauce before serving.

Griddle-Cakes (Lívance)

	Mix
25g yeast	with
70g sugar	until the yeast has liquefied. Sieve
300g flour	into a bowl, add the liquid yeast,
3 eggs,	
500ml milk	and work it into a runny batter. Leave to rise in a warm place, until it has doubled in volume. Heat a cast-iron pan for 10 minutes and grease it well with
fat.	Ladle the batter into the pan to make little cakes, about 10cm in diameter. Fry until golden, allowing 1-2 minutes for each side, and keep warm until all the cakes are ready. Grease the pan well after cooking each cake. When all the cakes are cooked, melt
100g butter,	pour it over the pancakes, stack them up and leave them in a warm place to steep for 10 minutes. Serve on a warmed plate and sprinkle with
60g icing sugar	and
1 level tsp	
cinnamon.	They can also be served with jam, "povidla" (plum jam), fresh blueberries, grated "tvaroh" (Czech curd cheese) or cream.

Plum Jam Turnovers (Povidlové taštičky)

Serves 6

	Sieve
300g flour	onto a pastry board. Add
1 egg,	
a little salt	and
4 tbsp milk	and quickly work the mixture into a firm pastry. Roll out the pastry to about ½cm thick and cut into discs about the size of the palm of the hand. Flavour
100g "povidla" (plum jam)	with
1 tbsp rum,	
a little cinnamon	and
sugar,	and spread equal quantities on each disc. Beat
1 egg	with a little water and brush around the edges of the pastry. Fold the pastry in half to form turnovers and press the edges together well. Put the turnovers into a pan of boiling salted water for about 6 minutes until they float to the surface. Remove them with a slotted spoon and rinse briefly in cold water. Dry and toss in
150g breadcrumbs.	Sprinkle with
2-3 tbsp icing sugar	before serving.

Plum Jam Turnovers

Ducat Cakes (Dukátové buchtičky)

	Thoroughly mix
25g yeast,	
50g sugar	and
a pinch of salt	until the yeast has liquefied. Briefly heat
100g butter	and pour on
250ml milk.	Sieve
500g flour	into a bowl. Add the milk, liquefied yeast and
3 egg yolks,	and work the mixture into a dough. Leave to rise for half an hour and then roll out on a floured pastry board to about a finger thick. Cut into small discs using a small glass or a pastry cutter. Place the cakes in a well greased baking tray and leave to rise for another half hour. Brush with
2 tbsp oil	and bake in a pre-heated oven at 200° for 30 minutes, until golden. Turn out while hot and sprinkle with
2 tbsp icing sugar.	Serve with hot custard, prepared as follows: Whisk
2 egg yolks	in
500ml milk,	and add
60g vanilla sugar	and
1 tbsp custard powder.	
	Place the bowl over a pan of simmering water and stir constantly until thickened. Finish with a dash of rum.

Ducat Cakes

Pancakes (Palačinky)

	Mix
200g flour	with
500ml milk,	
2 eggs,	and
1 pinch of salt	to form a smooth batter. Leave to stand for 20 minutes. Cook the pancakes in a lightly greased non-stick frying pan. Spread them with
4 tbsp jam,	roll them and sprinkle them with icing sugar. Palačinky are also delicious filled with fresh fruit or ice cream and topped with whipped cream.

Sunday "bábovka"

	Mix
25g yeast,	
40g sugar,	and
1 pinch of salt,	until the yeast has liquefied. Work
500g flour,	
4 egg yolks,	
100g butter,	
250ml milk	and the liquefied yeast into a soft dough. Knead
140g raisins	and
50 g slivered almonds	into the dough. Grease a kugelhupf mould (fluted ring shape) and sprinkle with
1 tbsp breadcrumbs.	Pour the dough into the mould and leave to rise for 30 minutes. Pre-heat the oven to 190° and bake the "bábovka" for 40-50 minutes. Sprinkle with
1 packet vanilla sugar	and
1 tbsp icing sugar	while still warm.

Bohemian Hotcakes (Vdolky)

	Mix
25g yeast	and
2 tsp sugar	until the yeast has liquefied. Sieve
400g flour	into a bowl. Add the liquefied yeast,
2 eggs,	
salt,	
250ml milk	and
1 packet of vanilla	
sugar,	and work into a dough. Leave to rise for 30 minutes then divide the dough into 8 pieces. On a floured pastry board, form each piece into a small loaf, then divide each loaf into small buns and leave to rise for another 15 minutes. Fry the buns in
300ml oil	in a large saucepan allowing about 4 minutes for each side. Drain briefly, top each bun with a little of
400g plum jam	or other preserve, and garnish with
400g quark ("tvaroh")	
(Czech curd cheese).	Serve immediately.

Bohemian Hotcakes

Prague Nut Cake (Pražský ořechový dort)

	Whisk
4 egg yolks	with
60g sugar	until frothy. In a second bowl, whisk
4 egg whites	and
a pinch of salt	until thick, gradually adding
50 icing sugar	to form a stiff meringue. Carefully fold this into the yolk mixture. Add
100g grated biscuits	and
100g ground walnuts	a spoonful at a time, and fold in along with
1 tsp baking powder.	Grease a spring form cake tin and sprinkle it with a layer of
breadcrumbs.	Pour the mixture into the tin and immediately put into a pre-heated oven at 170°. Bake for 35 minutes, leave to cool for a while, carefully loosen the edges and turn the cake out onto a wire cooling rack. When completely cool, slice in half with a long sharp bread knife. Whisk
150g butter	until frothy and gradually add
100g icing sugar,	
2 egg yolks,	
1 packet vanilla sugar	and
1 tbsp rum.	Spread it on the bottom half of the cake, place the other half on top and press down lightly. Mix
150g icing sugar,	
2 tbsp hot water	and
2 tbsp rum	into a smooth icing and glaze the top and sides of the cake with it. To decorate, whip
200ml whipping cream	with
2 tbsp icing sugar	and
1 tbsp cocoa powder	until thick, put into a piping-bag and, when the icing has dried, pipe 12 rosettes on top. Decorate the rosettes with
12 walnut halves	and leave to chill for 2 hours.

Prague Nut Cake

Christmas Cake (Vánočka)

	Soak
100g raisins	in
5 tbsp rum	and set aside. Mix
30g yeast	and
100g sugar	until the yeast has liquefied. Melt
200g butter	in a small pan and add
200ml milk.	Mix everything except the raisins into a soft dough with
500g flour,	
3 eggs,	
a pinch of salt	and
1 packet of vanilla sugar.	Knead the softened raisins into the dough with
120g slivered almonds	and
120g whole, blanched almonds.	
	The more you knead the dough now, the softer the cake will be later. The dough should be worked for at least 15 minutes then left in a warm place for an hour to rise. Divide the dough into three, roll out into strands about 40 cm long and plait together. Leave to rise for another 30 minutes. Brush with the yolk of
1 egg	and place on a greased baking tray. Bake for 50 minutes in a pre-heated oven on a high heat at first, then reduce the temperature.

Bohemian Shredded Pancake (Trhanec)

	Mix
250g flour,	
500ml milk,	
3 egg yolks	and
a pinch of salt	into a thin batter. You can also add
2 tbsp sugar.	Beat
3 egg whites	until thick and fold into the batter. Drain
500g sour cherries	and add to the batter along with
20g raisins.	Melt
50g butter	in a large frying pan and pour in the batter. After about 5 minutes, turn the pancake over and shred into large pieces with a fork. After another 4 minutes cooking time, put into a bowl and sprinkle with
2 tbsp icing sugar.	Serve hot.

Punch (Punč)

	Boil down
500g sugar	in
100ml water,	stirring constantly, until it starts to cara-melise. Add the juice of
3 lemons	and
1 orange,	remove from heat and pour in
400ml rum.	Stir well and serve hot in punch glasses. Any left-overs can be stored in tightly closed bottles and reheated. Do not allow the punch to come to a boil again when reheating.